Stroke This

My memoir account of my amazing recovery from a usually fatal, right sided paralyzing Pontine Infract brain stem hemorrhage stroke.

By Charles Firus

Acknowledgements

I want to thank the people who helped keep me on track to write this book.

I want to thank all my friends! They include Chris, Phil Z, Shelly, Larry, Mark, Rene', Bob and Trevor who all kept me going. Thanks Cathy, Jan, Joey D, Rick and others who visited me in the hospital

Thank you to my family members Including Karen, Trevor, Aunt Molly and Randi who have been great.

Thank You to my late Mother although very ill did the best she could under extremely difficult times after my stroke. She had to deal with as much as the care giver to me after my stroke.

Please forgive the grammar and spelling errors in this book. I have done it all by myself and this reflects who I am now.

Table of contents:

The Horror, The Horror

In the beginning, it was the best of times and the worst of times. It was around one in the morning on September 22, 2002. I had turned 46 that August in an instant my world as I knew it would change. I had a Pontine hemorrhage stroke this rendered me right side paralyzed. This was the least of my worries as I would soon find out. I had a Pontine Infarct that usually is fatal. This is a hemorrhage in the brainstem (the Pons) which is the switchboard to the entire brain. Breathing, heart rate, speech, vision, balance, muscle control, cognitive powers, everything that you can think of that makes us tick is routed thru the Pons. That's why about 75% of folks die the first day alone from this kind of stroke. I would say about 95% die by the end of the first week. I found this out three months after the stroke when I found out exactly what kind of stroke I had when I searched the internet for information. I found out that a Pontine stroke is one of the most devastating strokes to mankind plastered over dozens of websites.

I was paralyzed on the entire right side (slow to return) of my body. Plus being paralyzed, fighting back toward normality was the least of my problems and immediate issues. To explain all the stuff wrong with me is mind boggling and difficult to express and next to impossible for the average person to fully understand. Simplified, I should have died or at the very least been rendered severely disabled for a much, much, much longer time than I was. We're having some fun then! The effects of the stroke were beyond my normal comprehension of what a catastrophic event is, entails, and so on.

I worked very hard to a wonderful recovery which isn't easy by any stretch of the imagination easy especially considering the dark, negative, bitter attitude I had at the time right before the stroke. Certain friends thought. I was the most negative person they knew. I had made some improvements to myself in the 6 weeks before the stroke, but I was pretty much a wreck trying hard just to see the end of the tunnel, let alone trek past it. How then did I recover so well so far with a so called no positive attitude? Read on as plenty of my "manifesto" cracks open that crevasse of me, my soul that "made it happen".

Let's zip to the afternoon of stroke. I was tired from working that day. An AV "set up" of a general session audio visual show. But the day wasn't that stressful. The show must go on as Fred came over so we could do our radio internet sports who called "The Fred Johnson Sports Show" which we do for giggles. After the show

Fred and I had a few beers at the bar close by from my place in Huntington Beach. I was tired but wired when Fred went home. I went back to the bar for one last drink. Very tired I went home around midnight and watched T.V. until about one am on September 22, 2002.

I stripped naked and flopped toward the bed. Instead of taking off the ground and lying out on the bed, my right side completely collapsed. My right side crashed to the floor draping my still mobile left leg and arm on top of the bed. My paralyzed right side was "asleep" under the bed. I was not panicked or that concerned, thinking stupidly that this was temporary, that my right side was just "asleep" so too say. I was slightly struggled the first 15 then 30 minutes mostly resting. I kept thinking how tired I was and how I wouldn't be able to sleep for a while. My balance was completely shot, plus the world was spinning with extreme vertigo. I was very weak and used the bed and furniture as leverage to push myself inch by inch. I blew chunks if I moved more than a few inches at a time. I had no phone in my bedroom as the land phone was in my Parrot's room across the hall. The phone was connected to a long cord. My cell phone was left in the kitchen.

I guess you gather that moving was tedious. My head was facing and away from the direction I could partially move. I was very weak too. You know that! Yet I still didn't think I was that I was bad. Talk about denial or coping with the situation! My brain was in shock big time. I had to somehow spin my body around in limited space in the bedroom if I was to get out of my bedroom. I was extremely nauseous from the vertigo and unbelievable poor balance. Still, I didn't stay still, but pressed onward to get to a phone. I couldn't or didn't cry out loud enough to be heard by neighbors in the night. I was too polite! What an idiot I had become that night. The spins were ten times worse than your worse drunk ever could be. I used the bed and then my parrot Virgil's carrier cage for some kind of leverage to move. I knocked the cage to the floor and manipulated it in different spots between the wall and my good leg pushing and inching out of the room.

The night dragged on. I needed to relieve myself very bad. I lost control of my bladder. You can take a guess where I relieved myself. I also had thrown up perhaps five times during the multi-hours. I now was in the tiny hallway between my bedrooms, the bathroom, and my parrot's room where the phone was. Again, I was not panicked throughout the night and somehow thought I should piss in the toilet and not on myself. I had regained a tiny bit of strength and was pretty much "puked" out which somehow seemed to help. Talk about thirsty!!! I couldn't make it far in the bathroom and used the bathroom mat to spin me around on the floor with my head facing the hallway.

Over awhile, I managed to near Virgil's room as dawn was happening. Puddles of puke and piss I was now slithering in. I blew chunks one last time with only a ooze coming out. Ick! I was so thirsty. Dehydrated from throwing up everything I had up during the night. I was cold and didn't want to be found naked so I somehow put my bathing shorts on that I dragged with me out of my bedroom. I managed to drag the phone toward me with the cord. I couldn't or I wouldn't figure of too push 911 yet.

Then, I somehow gained a "second wind" and could raise to me feet and throw myself downward. I could move feet at a time. My mouth was so dry and my tongue so thick. I thought perhaps I could eat a piece of bread that I could reach. I couldn't swallow it. Somehow, I regained enough strength, in this a mind blowing effort, I rose like an accordion and flung to the ground multiple times and unlocked the front door as I knew I should try and negotiate the phone again for 911. I moved quickly compared to the 9 hours or so during the night. It still took a while to propel myself, bumbling and stumbling as I made it back to the phone. The print was big on the phone but it took me awhile to dial 911 correctly. I was so, so thirsty and disabled. I finally reached 911. My speech was so slurred from the stroke. Perhaps, I could finally get some water from the paramedics when they got there I thought. My mind was in shock with my cognitive ability shot, so I didn't think I was all that bad. I know what you're saying, "was I F-ing retarded"? All in all it was now after 10 am, pushing eleven. For 10 hours I had struggled to call the paramedics. This was the first of many sleepless nights too come.

It would be my first "ride" in an ambulance. The paramedics arrived within a few minutes after my call. "I've fallen and I can't get up" is what I slurred to the operator. I stayed on the line with the operator until the Huntington Beach paramedics arrived. About 3 paramedics arrived and after a consult with a doctor on their radio said it was a probable stroke that happened to me. I said "that makes sense". I hoped that my Virgil parrot would be okay. I couldn't really focus my eyes on him or anything for that matter during the ordeal. I could hear him chirp when I lay on the floor with my partial body in view of him when I pulled the phone cord earlier. I also purposely lay near where he could sort of see me when right before the paramedics came. I asked the paramedics to take my wallet and cell phone and to lock the door as they were placing me on the stretcher for my ride. I had a few times thought "taking the ride would be embarrassing in real life. I couldn't tell who saw me put into the ambulance. They would be taking me emergency in Newport Beach perhaps 5 to 6 miles away.

The emergency room was a nice 5 hour ordeal. I was able to call my mother who lived about 20 miles away in Anaheim with my choppy slurred voice. I wasn't sure she would come right away as she was in poor health herself. One of the nurses was kind enough to call Cathy who was my good friend and liaison work broker on the show. I was supposed to be doing free-lance audio visual for the rest of that week. The nurse called in sick for me. This was my first time calling in sick in two decades. Calling in sick was against my constitution. X-rays were in order for me, plus putting my body in the tube. At least they had a big tube barely big enough for me.

The 5 pounds I lost from my all-time high of 255 in the last 6 weeks wasn't a deal breaker with this tube. Still laying still was a problem. My body inside was rocking like a dingy in the stormy sea. What a rough shift. My mom arrived in what seemed like an eternity. I can't say they were in any hurry to move me to intensive care. They did their absolute best of not telling me anything other than I had a stroke.

Finally one nice attractive nurse told me" to listen to my nurses whatever I do" They were "riding" me to a different hospital. This was my insurance Primary care hospital. No one mentions ICU to me ever. The thumper called a defibrillator road on my gurney hugging my leg in the ambulance during my 8 mile or so ride. I had that warm and fuzzy feeling, not! Thump, Thump! I was very tired and rough when I got to the ICU. A lot of it was a blur literally. The stroke had left me ebbing and flowing with super things crashing and regaining some semblance of order.

I was in ICU three glorious days fighting for my life. It had to be at least a half dozen times that my pulse was crashing dropping below 50 sending the bells and whistles of my blue life signs machine to go off. A few times I was seriously thinking that that may be it as I was fading to oblivion for a tiny little while. I basically didn't sleep the whole time was there. I passed out, may have stopped existing "alive" for a few moments. I'm not sure, I haven't been able to get about 450 pages of my medical records. I've only seen 60 or so. I could hear other patients bells and whistles go off too adding to my fun.

My tongue was now thick and swelled as I have not drunk or ate anything since before the stroke. The nurse let me damp cotton swab the rough of my mouth but that was it. I had Severe tunnel vision was slowing dissipating after three days of ICU. My "spins" vertigo was still unbelievable but less after three days. No food or water after three days. I just had and IV in my arm. I was paranoid; nerves shot from the shock an extremely impaired invalid clinging to life. Oh yeah, I was still right side paralyzed on my entire right side with no movement return yet at all. My left side was affected too, bumbling and very weak. Amazingly, this negative soul remained positive and believed that I would not only live but recover well.

My first goal was to live to the next hour, than the next day. My will power had to be amazing. I was too frazzled, nervous and scared to sleep. I figured that folks died in their sleep and I couldn't "will" myself to stay alive asleep.

I had had the German measles as an adult 10 years earlier and couldn't sleep for nearly 5 days. Willing or controlling, even lowering my temperature when it creped really high. One time my temp snuck to 105.5 when I was too sick to monitor it.

I had numerous close calls fading away to death as I mentioned before. I was mentally prepared for death, but refused to accept the notion. I hadn't done crap yet with my life. I had no girlfriend, no beautiful wife, no house, no picket fence, and no mark on society. You know that feeling of purpose. I sure didn't want to be "out" at the age of 46. True, I didn't have much to live for, just my Parrot. But who would take him in? The only way death was in my mind was my thought to 100% positively prevents it from happening. I was thinking positive 100%. Not bad for an extremely negative person at the time of the stroke. The horror, the horror.

In The Woods

What a ride! No A ticket or E ticket or whatever they use these days. After three days of no real sleep, food, water, bathing and so on; I was finally out of the severe woods and transferred to the Dungeon for rehab. This was of speech, Physical and occupational therapy. Of course I wasn't really welcomed and laid ignored for hours alone. Where was my so called therapy plans listed on the chalk board that I was promised? After about twelve more hours of no sleep through the night that it was a "see if he survives before we do anything "kind of place. I could hear many patients in distress and heard one gentlemen die and his daughter distraught afterwards. The "Bells of Saint Mary's" were ringing all day all night. These were each individuals vitals machine is going off when they were in danger. I was next to the extremely noisy 24 hours a day nurses' station in critical Care. I couldn't read it on the door for weeks due to my really bad vision from the stroke. I did not sleep for the rest of the week. No doze off nothing. I was much too sacred of everything. I was still very bad off.

There were two of us to a room. The first night I thought someone was sleeping next to me. I don't know it was pretty dark. It was probably my imagination. The first day, my roommate had really bad knees and recent surgery on them. He was in severe pain. I thought he was asking for the black bottle or to cut them off to his wife and doctor. He wasn't there much longer. I still could hear machines bells ringing off and on all day long. I sing to you this melody!

This chapter might seem juxtaposed just like my scrambled mind! Where's the Teflon? Somewhere around the 5th day from the stroke I could move my leg a little. It was like pushing against a wall or trying to lift more than you can before I could move it inches. This effort was like trying to lift a thousand pounds. I got bowel control back the 4th or right now. The one thing I did was stay awake and drunk a mass amount of water. My tongue and esophagus were now not nearly so swollen so I could eat and drink. I was put on a strict 1,200 calorie diet. Talk about being weak. This lack of food sure didn't help. This sure beat the numerous tubes and tests I had to do it Intensive Care. What fun! And that bill keeps climbing! That defibrillator thumper pressed up against my leg each "ride". No one cared about my comfort. You got to love it! I'm paying for this? There goes my nest egg insurance or not!

At least my therapist Marco was going to start and get me walking with his assistant. I was all too excited!! This is a positive step (no pun intended). I walked with him maybe 50 feet the first day which was about five days after the stroke... I wanted more, but I'm sure Marco didn't want to kill me.

By trying really hard, by struggling painfully to move, as soon after a stroke as possible is the best way to help get movement back. This push, this pain trying to move went on and on and on for years since the stroke. Even now it still goes on. Less wrong with me now and less exertion and struggle all over the body, but still there along with that hole in my head. Folks often wondered if I had a hole in my head. Well yes! I'll have that hole forever!

Time was like insane the more ill I was. A minute seemed like an hour. It seemed like months and months maybe years for that first three weeks alone! Talk getting rid of that "time flies" feeling. It was a rough shift.

Oh yeah, that 1,200 calories a day diet? That diet includes Milk. I think that milk is barf time. I hate the smell, if I drink more than a few ounces I puke, barf, and throw up, blow chunks. They watched over me while I ate to see if I didn't choke and to track what I ate. Several times a day I was served milk I threw up many times as a kid as I was forced fed milk. Drink it. Drink it. Whole milk whole fatty milk is the worse. I told the hawk girl therapist every single time, did I say single time? I told them that milk made me puke and to substitute it. I was given that "right" sound, humoring me and not really believing me. God this sucked, failing to complete nearly every meal. I was a failure eating 1,200 calories a day. Sure they were tiny 6 ounce cartons of milk wasted nearly every meal, but I ate less those 1,200 calories a day. I was a big boy weighing 250 pounds at the time of the stroke. I was so weak trying to move parts that didn't move I tried constantly, constantly, constantly, constantly! Above everything, as I found out later they had no idea that I wasn't sleeping although monitored and checking, and drawing blood every 4 hours. The dungeon was a vampires dream.

Oh yeah, When I was finally able to shower/bath after 5 days from the stroke I was helped (really mostly watched) by a "girl" occupational therapist shower. I struggled to even sit under the water. This striped of shame and dignity being naked in front of her. So at least I was clean!

Around that time I got to brush my teeth for the first time since the stroke. This was the first time in over 5 days. Yes, you remembered, puke still in my mouth from the night of the stroke and remnants of milk!!!!!!!!!!!!!!!!!!!!!! Ugh!!!!!!!!!!!!!!!!!!!!! I had a chance I thought for survival by now.

Nobody in general told me anything except the obligatory "rah speech" by head doctor. He said I could get better with a lot of hard work and recover well. The more you try to move and move, the more you are likely to improve. I liked this because effort was my strong suit in life. This was what I was very, very, good at. I really tried hard at things in general. This is my curse that leads to my downfall. I tried and cared too much. I internalized too much and tried too hard until I gave up basically the last few years to the stroke.

Trying really hard all my life got me little in life. I perceived that most did not care and if anything I was "usable" too do more, way more in work. I'll stop rambling now, but I knew that I worked harder than most all my life. I could get better and beat the odds, if I didn't croak in the next few weeks or months. Many still do as I suspected and figured out later. Let's talk brain damage. Besides my brain damage," that will leave a mark", "that's going on your permanent record" whole in my head; what I'm trying to say is: My mom grabbed and took my cell phone away early into this ordeal. How's that for a scrambled sentence. I wondered why? I saw it as negative and like most things since the stroke I did not have that warm and fuzzy feeling. I told her that all my phone numbers were in this and I needed them, that they could speed dial, and that my vision was impaired and this made it easy on me and felt more secure to me. She gave no answer the whole time (no pun intended) or ever for that matter. Gees, I saw it as "let's give up on him", "he's going to die and doesn't need it" attitude from her. I perceived not only give up from her every second every day, but that gloom "he's dead (dying) but doesn't know it yet" attitude. Everything she said was construed by me as negative. She would take paper work forms for disability away from me. She didn't see me trying to fill them out, intact with my memories, worth living person. I saw her as a "pull the plug and let him die" kind of person.

Her father had died from throat cancer at 46 when she was a young girl, and she assumed I was going to die. Guess what! I was 46! This daily reminder of doom and gloom was not good for me. I couldn't understand her crises management. She was very ill herself and thought she was doing what was right and best for me, but I thought it and it was the exact opposite of her intent. I had/have dozens of examples but I won't beat a dead horse. Talk about hurdles and road blocks, everywhere!

I want to make it clear that my many friends who saw me were positively fantastic! They were great. Chris, Rene', Jan and Cathy were great every time. My aunt Terry and Uncle Bob were great as well as my cousin Randi. You get the picture. I could see night and day difference between my Mother's and brother's attitudes perceived by me and everybody else. This was paramount! The biggest differential I've seen in my life. Was I crazy? What weren't they telling me? What wasn't my mom telling me? What weren't the doctors telling me? Their best quality was giving no or little information? What didn't my friends know? I knew my chances of survival were poor. Did I really need the famous quote from my Mom to me "You don't know how sick you really are!!!!" What a statement haunting me. What aren't they telling me? I thought I could beat a thousand to one chance of survival, but what else broke? Did I have failing organs or something like that?

This made things even harder. I was showing so much improvement. Yet, I was still so very ill.

So many things helped secure my nervousness. By the time I showered I had a new roommate. He was 54 and had diabetes since a child. He was talking with his wife and pausing for five seconds in the middle of a sentence. I called it blanking out. His doctor came in to talk and said directly to him, "how long have you had congestive heart failure? He said back, "I didn't know I had congestive heart failure". What????????????????????? How is this possible? How couldn't he know probably for week's even months!! He was soon wheeled away never to return or seen by me again. I figured it was to the "death room" and the place to die. So many folks died in the dungeon.

Oh Hell, let's make it everybody!!! So many victims with their machines ringing their pending doom. Did I have shit wrong that they weren't telling me? My mother said "you don't know how sick you really are" to me. Ring the church bells don't you think I felt/knew/assumed my survival was very difficult. Don't you think I knew I was supposed to be dead already? Don't you think my body was in havoc internally? I was much, much, much more lucid and aware than I was given credit for, or so it seemed to me. Yes my body was very impaired and I was a weak invalid including speech, but it was Charlie and I was aware. My hearing seemed bionic and I remembered and perceived so much clinging onto life. I kept trying to move parts that didn't move with the parts that did move. This reminder would help my muscles remember. This helped to keep my pulse up when it was failing away to oblivion. I continued with no sleep. I had my television on all the time. It was on 24 hours a day.

I so appreciated the day when many of my friends came to visit me at the same time of day. Dave, Kevin, Rick and others. What a treat. Days later, maybe a week or so Joey D. came to visit.-I cherish all the visits. I was visited by Rene' and Chris every day. There were many visits to me by Cathy, Jan, Uncle Bob and Aunt Terry. I appreciate my visit from my cousin Randi so much. The memories are still clear even now 10 years since the stroke. How's that for a dummy? I remember the time of day on many events.

Oh "he's crazy" the common thread. The therapy staff was very helpful to me. I thought the nurses and doctors were not helpful. I could hear all the crap and negative comments delivered at the nursing stand to each other. I heard the battle-axe rants at night to a new hire nurse. I heard talk of poor survival, alright death, no pussy footing around that they would say, including making a clunking noise on each file as she would say, "Dead, Dead, Dead, Dead, Dead!" Those were obviously due to die. Was I included? You bet you baby!!!!!!Was I tunes/crazy/loony/nuts? No, I don't think so. There was so much evidence after days. It has been is only five days from the stroke. I was near death no doubt! This alone isn't good for you short term or in the long run.

Once Upon A Late Night Dreary

I am now in day 6 on a Friday. I am determined to live. I want to live, but what isn't wrong with me? The hemorrhage was in the Pons in the brain so I found out three months later. No one, no doctor, no nurse, nobody told me where, and above all what to expect.

The pons is really the switchboard/router of the brain. All parts of the brain signal travels through the Pons. Therefore not only was I right sided paralyzed, but my left side was affected to. Plus my breathing, heartbeat, temperature control, and you name it were disrupted. Everything in my body was affected. That is why websites say that a Pons stroke is one of the most devastating strokes to mankind. It is "invariably fatal". We're talking a high chance of dying in the first week alone. At least 90 % die from a Pons stroke in the first week. Even if you live, only some fight back to some normal sense of normal. Many are rendered lifetime invalids or never get out of a wheel chair!

I knew nothing of this then, but knew even if I was now a million to one to live I was going to do it. There was all the death around me, and that one statement by my

Mother, "you don't know how sick you really are!" Sure she meant well and I love her, but this one statement created my fear. It appeared that many people were not really on my side to live!!!! All of this the hours and days of stuff made me figure I was worse than a thousand to one to live. The reality was I was probably at least even money by now to live. Something else besides the stroke had to be wrong with me. This so called problem was caused by the stroke and was concealed from me. In a way I didn't want to know as I was 100% positive I would fight and somehow live.

I did not talk of death and negative things to people about my estate such as my pet parrot Virgil. Not at all until my rant to Rick who came to visit me on Friday with his girlfriend. I'm sure I talked in riddles and was far from clear but I told him to make sure they do an autopsy on me. I feared that I would be killed. You know pull the plug on me or given the black bottle (poison) or a fatal injection. You name it. I had tried so very hard to stay alive so far. I couldn't risk tint chance that they were killers.

No sleeping yet. I didn't trust more than half the people in the dungeon. The twisted night staff had continued evidence piling up against me. I didn't know whether some were really evil or just playing games on who would die next. I literally heard the staff discuss evil whispers outside my door by the famous nurse's stand. I was now living a horror movie. Did the staff do euthanasia on the patients? My ears were bionic to the whispers. The tunnel vision was now gone and the vertigo gone. I was improving in so many ways!

I heard paramedics and the death wagon coroner people called several times during nights. I could hear the setup of their equipment. I could hear so much easier at night.

There was so much less overall background noise. The death wagon people would take the fresh dead away. I could hear the respirator stop on patients several different times the past few nights. I could hear the beeping, the sound big vehicles make when in reverse and backing up. I know this sound all too well as I hate this sound for the last few decades and I've hated that tune playing over and over to me hundreds of times. And there is little chance of being wrong. I could hear vehicle engines at night. I could still hear the staff plotting what can be construed as "conspiring to kill" for the last few nights. I had no faith in the evening and night staff but one male nurse I think him name was Angel. He had a rougher Andy Garcia look. He was truly kind by his actions. There was so much building up and I had no real sleep now for 6 long days and night. It seemed like months. I'm sure I was considered delusional in general. "Oh, he thinks he's going to live and recover. They think to themselves as Dr. Evil in

Austin powers "Right" Lack of sleep alone can make you temporarily: I was a cracker / tunes / nuts and for coco puffs crazy!!!! Whispers cry out for attention. Whispers, I overheard or partially heard so much even in the days. Every day I could hear someone say "no way" as for my survival.

I had a new roommate name Phil. He was 60, but looked 75. He was found near death in his home from ailments, a failing heart and longtime alcoholism. He wanted booze and morning coffee. He was clueless to how sick he really was. He was a day from death, Perhaps they can get him running for a week. He hadn't been eating when home before the dungeon He was stubborn and not the right guy too keep the peace.

Bon appetite, the food served came into play! The evening and night staff was to wacky to 100% believed. I knew rationally that they were probably okay but I was wary. I could take no chance if they were screwing with my life and survival! It seemed to me from the data compiled that they were screwing with the food. Dig this, on the six day a Friday there was a different Nutritionist. Oh that night in the dungeon. I had an evening snack given to me for the first time. This was on top of my 1,200 calories. I wasn't going to eat it. I was too scared of that the paper thin snack would kill me! I got a call from the nutritionist speaking loudly to me. Mr. Firus don't eat the snack! You're not supposed to eat the snack. He sounded panicked raising my suspicions like heated yeast!

Then, I could hear whispering willow euthanizes. Hey, I wanted to live!! It sounded like one of staff said "what's it in today"? Then a male conspiring nurse came in a shook Phil awake. He said loudly with a fake smile, "How about a nice sandwich Phil. You want a nice sandwich." I thought they were offing right next to me. I could barely sit up with all my balance so far from normal it's unbelievable. Sure the vertigo was gone but this balance really bad. If I took a step and fall on my own. How could I help Phil? How could I get out of there? How can I trust the food and water? How was I supposed to last the night? 6 days and nights without sleep were getting to me. I shook from the severe weakness, poor balance, being paralyzed, and the romper room in my organs. I was shaking the night away and the shock of the stroke. Whammy, things don't look good! The male nurse left and Phil quickly fell back asleep snoring loudly! Sleep...wasn't on my mind.

I hope you like my convoluted, juxtaposed and fragmented style! See.... I can use big words! Supercalifragilisticexpialidocious! I was scared. It was only 9:00 pm. How was I going to make it to 6:00 am and the day shift? Why did my Mom take my cell phone? I dialed my room phone to try and make a call. It was routed through the nursing stand. I could hear the battle axe nurse hang-up my call and then her phone sending the dial tone to me. She knew it was me. I am now in day 6. I am determined to live! I want to live, but what isn't wrong with me? I was so very tired but very wired. Good God this sucked. I needed help but I didn't know how to ask for help. I never did ask for help in all my years in School. This was a foreign subject to me.

I was lying in bed with my bed with front raised to a pretty good angle. It was "like" sitting in a chair. Each day in the dungeon I raised it up more and more. I did not lay flat at all since I was in Intensive Care. I was staying awake ready for action and ready to fight death. My paralyzed right side was close to the open door smack in front of the nurse's stand. Room 212! Phil snored to the right of me to. My movable side was close to the window outside. The window had small frames in it was really only a foot of window to sneak by breaking and squeeze through. The odds of this escape were low as it was a nice drop into the slopping ivy below. Why did my movable side have to be farthest from blocking the murders? I had to keep trying to make calls when the battle station ruined by the battle axe was vacant! I had to get out of there so I could get some sleep. I knew I had to start sleeping some!

Beep, beep, and beep, out goes the light. It was dark in my room. This was to keep prowler, stumbling, holocaust skinny Phil asleep. The room door was always open to the lighted hall. This door never closed. They might as well axe it away. My small TV two feet from my head kept me somewhat lit with off and on shadows. It was on the right side so it was a partial block of the predators!

Finally, it seemed like the battle axe was on lunch break and the coast was clear of staff. I dialed Rene and it went through. I could hear the phone ring. Rene answered it as it was well into the night like two am. I told him briefly what I thought and he assured me things were alright and to go asleep. Sleep? What's that? I was less panicked for a while.

The night wore on and continued to wear me out. The odds were low that they were killers, but I couldn't trust them! I called my mother around three am. She ranted at me and said "what am I going to do with you?" She was absolutely scaring me worse. It was like lying on a bed of nails and seeing the guillotine axe fall! She was the opposite of help. She was uneasy and spinning me out of control. I don't need somebody irritable! Was she part of it? I'm still floating here! I was worthy of living! Who are these people making decisions?

My anxiety and fear was busting like a balloon! I have never reached this kind of fear before like during the next hour. I Heard whispers and gloomily lit shadows piercing my statue fear skin. Beep, Beep, Beep as the death wagon took another stiff away!!! The conspiracy continued with the grassy knoll of evil outside my door. Boy was I frightened. The nurses were back and ready! My eyes were bug eyed and peeled to the door of my room. I sensed that one would about to enter praying on the weak. She briskly walked in without a word severely over weight with a fat ass. She seemed to have something in her hand slightly concealed. Perhaps it was a needle in her hand. This all happened quickly! She traversed half the distance to my bed staring at me and saying nothing!

I screamed at the top of my lunges sentences blurred together. "Stay away from me"!!!! I rose up in the bed blurting loudly. I was going to fight for my life. She paused and stopped and sat on the corner of Phil's bed hiding her hand. She was rational. She asked me if I wanted to hurt myself. I yelled "no, the opposite I want to live!!!" "Don't touch me" I yelped. I think she wanted to call the police as I did not want to be there anymore. I said something to the effect, "go right ahead". This was scarier than anything ever before to me.

My whole life the last six days of the struggle was to stay alive. The last six days without real sleep. It was now four am. She finally left for reinforcements or to regroup. Phil was snoring and out. He slept like a rock throughout this! Wow, how intense!!!! I could hear some commotion in the hall and soon heard sirens. The sirens became louder and I knew they were coming because of me. Blow the party favors! I'm busted for the first time in my life by the man! Two policemen arrived and were in the hall. The night male nurse and I chatted. One cop there too. I seemed rational to them. I explained that I figured from all my so called over hearing "evidence" that I couldn't trust that I wasn't going to get clipped.

Before too long ambulance thugs came to take me away. I wasn't clear where but away from the dungeon and the night shift was fine by me. Long live sleep deprivation! It was still dark, on a late September night/morning. It was pushing 5 am by now. The ambulance parked in stone throwing distance of another really big hospital which I could sort of see through the misty fog. I was kicked to the curb! I finally got to lay in the gutter! It was a big night for firsts. There I played on a really short legged gurney gutter water splashing, cool brisk weather a tiny blanket and my nightie on bare legged. My mom and the shrink arrived at the same time.

Now I Lay Thee Down To sleep

I needed sleep so badly! The stroke was on Saturday was a week ago. Technically, the stroke was during the night at one am Sunday morning. It was now the next Saturday morning 6am. I had not really slept since the Friday night the week before. Way past what you should do if you are fine. You're loony after these 7 days without real sleep. I knew I had to get some sleep. The last time was on Tuesday but after the transfer from intensive care to the dungeon. I was too scared and rattled. My nerves were beyond shot and I thought maybe they were out to kill me! The heartbeat goes on.

Where's Tony De Franco when you need him? How about Joey Buttafucco? My tail was between my legs with my open air back and ass hanging out as my gift to the world.

I was finally wheeled in building which was a new hospital! And then, trumpets please.... I was left in the hallway to the emergency room with no explanation. There was no one in site in the secluded hallway. I was left in the hall with time ticking. Something was draining into my bloodstream. Crap! I was off IV since Wednesday! Hour by hour went by. I really feared death so I continued to fight sleeping. You die in your sleep!!!! I was still in the hallway with little following up by the staff for hours. You got to love it!

Time kept on ticking for me in that unpopulated hallway. It was actually was pretty quiet I think. I could not sleep.

I couldn't chance it. I was determined to beat this drug dripping in my arm. Some nondescript staff dropped by and wheeled me in a tiny heavily windowed tiny, tiny room. I would say I was left alone awhile. I was still in the hallway with little following up by the staff for hours. It was more than awhile. I remember nobody there. No bells and whistles and that darn blue vitals reading box. I had that liquid dripping in my veins. Comforting! Not!

Low and behold my cousin Randi appeared at my side. She said she was coming to see me today earlier in the week when she was out of state in Washington D.C. She was like an angel for my determined desperate eyes. It was fantastic to see her and re-energized me. If that was really possible then! I stated that I didn't want a sedative. At least I think so. If I only knew it was OK to sleep. If I only knew that a lot of things were ok. Hindsight we are geniuses. I needed a break from the stress. Randi was so calm and together. She was so soothing. Just what I needed a calming source and to be away from the dungeon.

I didn't get breakfast in new emergency hall. No water, no lunch either. Time became the afternoon. Wonderful Hospitality....NOT! I was paying for this along with Blue Cross. What a shame. I was stored there like lumber. Will he go to psych still? Will he ever get a room? Will he go some other place that doesn't want him? Yet, I had some peace in that glass closet. I was there glass menagerie! Shaw or Spock? That's enough of that "Give me liberty or give me death"

Crap!

The day lived on whether I was cared for or not. It was deep into the afternoon. Was I dying or falling asleep? I didn't know for sure. At least I felt better with Randi there. I was finally taken upstairs where a doctor looked at me as if I was crazy for loudly claiming I wanted to live!!!I did not want to fill out the forms or sign away my life with that "do not resuscitate" junk. I knew she thought I was insane. Sure enough a year later when I saw 60 pages of my 450 pages of medical files she proclaimed me with a wrong diagnosis of me. My god she didn't even know what was wrong with me. And she now was in charge of my life!

I was placed in a private room and the first thing I could see was a Christian Cross on the wall. I could view it over my feet from my new bed. No food yet. But I had Jesus and what I figured I was in the death room!!! I didn't even get a last meal! Just a diaper! I haven't been wearing a diaper for many days, I went number two in the bathroom at the dungeon before I freaked. Randi was still there! Soon Rene and his wife carol showed up. I was glad to see them. I was scared to go to sleep.

Somewhere in here Randi left and a "in room male attendant/nurse "came in my room. I was finally fed around this time. It was beef stroganoff. I was offered a second meal and I took it. I hadn't eaten the last 25 hours. Somehow I thought I was blowing my diet. Not a bad last meal I thought. Interesting thing is on the night my Father passed away I had a beef stroganoff TV dinner for Supper. Hmmmmmmmmmmmm! Interesting! And this fact was clear in my mind as I wolfed down the irony!!! Somewhere in here I was strapped down to the bed. This was not comforting to me but the opposite. I didn't need that shit to be tied or the diaper. I could pretty much stare at the cross on the wall and the TV. Rene convinced me to go to sleep that I was not dying. No sleep for me yet. I was tied down to my bed and imprisoned by my all night Jamaican male nurse. He was pleasant. Rene left around 6pm. Time crept toward 9pm and the room was pretty dark but the TV. The nurse was snoring away and I was finally calming down. Now I lay me down too sleep at about 9:20pm. It was nearly 8 days from the stroke. This was the first real sleep I had gotten since the stroke!

NEW DAWN

It was the first night sleep since the stroke a week ago. The split second I woke up I checked to make sure I didn't have tubes sticking out of my neck for breathing. Nope. I did have that dripping in my hand still and had tiny nasal oxygen tube in my nose I think. Actually, I woke up when it was still dark at 4:20am. I slept for about six hours. Yippee! Finally! I felt tons better. The Jamaican male nurse was still snoring away. No bells and whistles of my vital machine went off all night. At least that I knew of! I made it! I sure needed I needed to sleep since Tuesday after I got out of intensive care. It was now Sunday. The stroke was a week ago Friday Night.

So here I was in a new unimproved hospital. Things have reverted back to a diaper and no physical therapy. Of course the sooner you try to move and move what you can the better chance that your brain will remember and rewire over time to improve. Of course I was doing number 2 in the restroom at Tustin. Of course I continued shaking my good leg and moving or trying to move what I could. To me trying to get the paralyzed side to move was like weight lifting more than you can do. It is like trying to push over a wall. Slowly after many attempts and much effort and will power parts begin to move ever so slightly and slowly. By this time I could raise my right X-completely paralyzed right leg slightly in the air. Movement comes back closer to your body center first.

Of course I still figured I was scheduled to die by the upper command doctors. Of course this chapter should be called Of course instead of New Dawn. This New Dawn was special for me because some of the fear and so much of the indescribable exhaustion were gone from my snooze.

They didn't give a crap about a 1,200 calorie diet at St. Josephs. I'm just diapered up, no therapy to help me move at Joe's. I'm just lying there to crap my pants and stare at that cross on the wall in front of me. "I was living the dream, Jerry, I was living" as George Costanza said. I was living the dream left for dead and watching TV with my much impaired vision. The tunnel vision was gone. The "spins" vertigo was gone, but the room swayed way more than a drunk Robert Shaw in Jaws. My balance was beyond pathetic still, but not as bad as it was last week. I was so much better than a week ago, but still ridiculous to think I was scheduled to live.

The Calvary arrived about 10:00 am. It sure didn't hurt getting that positive vibe from my Uncle Bob and Aunt Terry. They were so fantastic. I showed them how much I could lift my ounce paralyzed leg. Perhaps 12 to 15 inches off the bed, not Johnson inches either! I could lift from the thigh first of course. It was a wonderful half hour to an hour visit. Time flies when you're having fun or some face simile!

The day wore on and I was offered "the chance" to go back to Tustin. I knew that Joe's was not the answer as far as moving therapy and trying to recover as fast as I could. Remember, the more you try to move early after a stroke the better chance for a good recovery. I really needed to recover. I was pumped for it!!!! My head was clearer now, but still I was afraid of the future back at the dungeon. I was going back there for keeps. Bring the napkins to the picnic! My ride arrived, no sound screaming sirens, just the thumper, gurney and two dudes. It was Sunday and Sunday night is a ghost town of staff at my destination Tustin.

I knew it would take a long herculean effort to get better. I didn't know just how very, very, very hard it would be. I had all that effort with such a little improvement each day. After all "tomorrow is a new day"! I could use another night's sleep but I was returning to Tustin. The odds of sleeping tonight are let me say: "Not going to happen, got to be prudent! Got to stay alive another day. "I was nervous more about the staff eliminating from the living. See my level of confidence of survival?

It was quiet, seemed empty of staff and just like a horror movie. I was put in the same room with Phil already sleeping. My vision was tunneled no more and the nasty vertigo was gone. I could see a bit better and comprehend surroundings better. You guessed it; there was no way I was going to sleep that night. I needed day light, staff and Monday morning coming down. It was another new dawn with the routine of getting everybody Up. Every bloody day! I hate mornings! The nurse takes my blood every six hours. Please charge me for everything! The morning wasn't so bad as usual because I didn't sleep. I welcomed the morning sun light to add more visual awareness against possible attacks against me. I would need to bite the bullet again and pretend to trust these people. I did have a beginning acting class in college!

I still drank plenty of water. Way more than plenty of water! A few times I drank right out of the tap in the rec room. I would be the only one in there early in the morning. I wheeled myself to the rec room in my chair. I continued therapy in walking with assistance and trying to move more. Trying to move is like pressing as hard as you can for prolonged time to try and get that muscle to move. It is like trying to lift a thousand pounds!!! This effort will happen tens of thousands of time. Many painful efforts and many days/months/years to accomplish getting movement back. I am still working out kinks!!!

I am skipping too much in future months here as I really only had a little movement in my right thigh. A glimmer of hope presented to me on my right sided paralyzed side a week after the stroke. There was so much wrong with me being paralyzed was the least of my worries. I didn't go home on Tuesday as promised. The doctors argued over my care. I would stay at the rehab dungeon! I was still rattled and scared. I only slept about every third night. I still thought I was scheduled to die. What weren't they telling me? I was told very little by anybody. Let me say that again. I was told very little by anybody. I was left in the dark.

My gloom Mother and Brother only made things worse. My Mother had the hospital Chaplain stops by. I didn't need that! I was positive I was going to live and recover! I did not have any talk of death or dying with anyone. It was a pleasant generic talk with the chaplain.

I was getting less weak daily. I was less invalidly. I'm sure that's not a word. I continued my therapy on trying to move with very minor progress for the last two weeks in the dungeon. I spent half of my time in a wheel chair. Rene, Chris, and Jan came so many days. Rene sees me every day! I was so grateful for all their support. Cathy wheeled my wheel chair outside in the courtyard one afternoon. It was so wonderful for me to be outside! I had enough faculties to smell the roses!

I will spare you the details with all my struggles those final weeks in the hospital. 21 to 22 days in all in the hospital. They were finally letting me out. I was so tired and scared. I wanted to leave desperately. The head doctor wanted to talk me into another week, but I really had to get out of there. I finally voiced to my Mother that I had hardly slept for three weeks and I was moved to a quieter room away from the noisy nurse's stand. I slept great in my new room. Three cheers to me for finally going home! Well, my Mom's apartment.

Don't Fold Bend Or Mutilate

"Charlie gets out of the hospital for what?" I spouted out! I was to be going home after 22 days of wishing I was out of the hospital. I really wanted to see my Parrot Virgil. I missed him terribly and only hopes he was well at Cathy's house. She wouldn't really mention anything about him seems to me so was he still alive? Did he fly away? Was I supposed to be dead? Don't worry about him. If I thought time nearly stood still before waiting for my Mom to come pick me up in the morning was so hard. She seemed to take hours longer to arrive with my brother I think? Did he hide in the corner? It seems like he was there. My Mom need to sign all the paperwork and it seemed like days as she read and signed. I couldn't believe it. She was so angry at me for wanting her to hurry up in her typical apathetic way. Did she say hello? This was my perception anyway. What do I know; I have a hole in my head! I was beyond desperate to leave. She was ill and seemed more oblivious than me.

That's saying something. We were both on one track ideas that were on opposite ends of the Earth. She wanted to take her time and could have no distractions and no asshole giving her the bums rush.

Well!!!!!!!!!!!!!!!!!! This was the big foreshadow! There was no marching band. No parade. No banner. No welcome home asshole or should I say welcome home Son. I'm so proud of you. No, not that. There was no joy in Mudville! No joy from my Mother or Brother. Nothing! Mighty Casey had struck out. He lived. He's going home to her place. I needed a caregiver on the first floor. Is there care in caregiver? I was a burden to her. I was nonexistent to my Brother. I was supposed to die in the hospital and was not coming home. My perception is she was quickly giving up even more on me. Oh that hole in the head! Man, perceptions suck!!!!!! Hey, hey, I'm foreshadowing now! There was a lot of bickering while easing me in the car. I wasn't made of eggs. This is natural to "over" stress when dealing with a near invalid.

It was good to see the trees as we drove. My vision wasn't that bad now. It was neat being out of Tustin and being on the streets again. Just let me chill at my Mom's place. We arrived and my wheel chair was poorly moved out of the car. Wow can I not take agitation in my rattled, nerves and fried mind. Please stay calm and let me chill. Don't panic! You should try and keep me calm.

Don't worry banging me around just don't panic. Entering my Mom's apartment was interesting. My brother Paul was semi-living there between jobs on the couch. It had one bedroom. I said I wanted no big deal or effort by Paul. Paul in his crazed hurry and bumble mood immediately started in the bedroom and started rearranging everything. I couldn't stand the noises, banging, grunts, yelping continued for what had to be over an hour. I wanted none of this. No noise.

He moved the TV so I could see it from my Mom's hospital bed in her bedroom where I would be sleeping. I couldn't care less at this juncture. Don't ask the patient what he wants or needs! Once again I had no fanfare and no nothing. There was a lot of bickering between my brother and mom. I wanted to sleep so badly by afternoon. This every three days the last two weeks had to stop! They screamed and yelled how difficult the wheel chair moved on carpet. This had to change. They were ridiculous. I wanted to get up and crawl to the restroom. This was insane moving me Paul or my Mom. Paul would not listen to a word I said "Ahhhhhhhhhhhhhhh! Are you kidding me? I struggled to live for this?"

Finally, I got into bed. My mom's hospital bed she normally sleeps in. I would have slept on the couch. It has an attached control remote to raise or lower the top half or bottom half of the bed. They left me. They left me to argue actually. A drag out yelling fight occurred as Paul was preparing to leave. He had to get a job, blah, blah, blah. So much for me trying to get sleep any time soon. What a joke. Many minutes passes as they yelled. I figure on adjusting the bed to raise it higher on the torso side like I had been sleeping since intensive Care. 18 days I think. I started pressing a button or two and much to "my sue-prize and dis-o-may" the bed began to close in on me. Both ways bending me in two, squeezing me together!!! I faintly yelled out. I needed more volume to be heard from the screaming argument in the next room. I fumbled and bumbled with the buttons on the remote as the bed slowly was sandwiching me. Finally, I got it to stop and managed to get it to reverse toward normal!!

What an ordeal! I got out of the hospital for this! Somewhere the band was playing...There was no joy in Mudville! I really didn't sleep that night. I was to wound up from the commotion. Perhaps 20 minutes. I could hear my Mom's walk clock ticking all night. I can't stand the "time Bomb" ticking sound. That clock had to go tomorrow!

My Mom as you know by now is really ill and her wits and strength is really. On top of all this, is that my brother Paul is really depressed and between jobs. Well, morning has broken, blackbird has not woken. It is just my 1,200 calorie a day diet to look forward to food wise!

I think it was this day that I hoped Cathy would bring my pet parrot Virgil to me. Remember she was keeping care of him for me. I hoped he was alright as I loved him and I missed him so. I hoped he was alright and still alive! First comes moving me and my wheelchair around on the carpet this was next to impossible, Semi-walking with my 4 prong cane was next to impossible on the carpet. I felt like I was moving in glue barely being able to lift my feet! Wow! I had to look forward to that hearty breakfast! It felt more comforting knowing I was away from the fear of being clipped in the hospital. One battle to fight and win at a time! It is so good to be alive! Afternoon had started and sometime soon Cathy would be bringing my Parrot Virgil to me.

Time wasn't standing still for me anymore. Let us say I really wanted Virgil to be with me again maybe a half hour or so after she was due to arrive with Virgil the knock on the one bedroom apartment. The door opened and Cathy came in along with my friend Nader carrying Virgil's cage with Virgil in!!!!!!!! I was so glad. I was sitting on the coach and Nader placed his cage on something like a shelf above my head on my right side. After joyous greetings I stretched and snapped open the clasp that held his cage shut. Cathy said, "Oh that opens". She had been struggling sliding with the little windows to feed him and give him water for the last 2 weeks. Virgil stood in his fence post mood not knowing what to make of everything. He was in his figure things out mode and of course saw me severely impaired.

Virgil was fence posting for about 20 minutes it seemed as Nader, Cathy, and my Mother talked. He finally, for no apparent reason ducked his head in his seldom done "pet my head" pose to me. I had to really stretch and what seemed like a long time to stretch a few feet to scratch the feathers (pet) on his head. This was so precious too me. It's good to alive!!!!

One Step at a time

It was good to have some control on things, but still so much medication and 1,200 calories a day. Good God I was hungry. My nerves were still shot to hell. I slowly improved. Always trying to move the right side and moving the left to remind the right side. This was going to be a long time to get back toward normal. Yes for months and months, years and years. You got to keep moving!!! I would get home physical therapy a few times a week for 6 weeks I think from my insurance. Jerry was his name and started my home workout routine with me. I walked with the cane every day.

It was so hard on the carpet but easier on the outdoor hallway cement. It was good to have some control on things, but still so much medication. Things hurt. My heart felt like it was beating out of my chest. Really heavy on my ribs causing pain and I didn't know if this was really bad or not. It was improbable for me to calm down and not be so nervous with high pulse.

I really needed peace but there was little at my Mother's apartment. I hated the clock ticking along with the slight noise of the air purifier. My Mother had hard time breathing and often ran the insanely noisy kitchen stove fan. Somehow she thought she got more oxygen this way but this was killing my head and nerves which no longer existed. I was shell shocked toward nothing. I could move a tiny bit now with extreme effort!!!

"Just one Tylenol" was my Mother's amazing ridiculous statement to me. What? "Just one Tylenol all day" I thought. "The doctor said just one" She is hard of hearing and is illogical. I hurt real badly. I hurt in my chest. There is no way I could only take one Tylenol all day! She refused to give me more. I was too weak to get it myself. She honestly thought this was right. I suffered for hours leading to days. Thanks Mom. This is one of hundreds of examples of lack of communication, illogical events leading to more suffering for me.

After about two weeks at home and about 5 weeks from the stroke I was scared that something maybe wrong with my heart and that insane beating and pressure on my chest. I was up to 1,500 or so calories a day from my doctor visit a week before. This day I couldn't stand it anymore; my brother drove me to emergency where they of course admitted me. I still knew shit. I still thought I was due to die and was not being told this. Why couldn't I get any comforting information? Well, how about three days in the hospital running tests with absolutely no information. I was scared shirtless being back. Of course I got nothing to relax me or calm me down. Gees, this is so hard? Was my heart ready to go bye bye? I would keep fighting although very scared.

A messed up mind analytical side of the brain totally shot to H. All kinds of things were slow and a struggle. I usually put my shirt on backwards. This haunted me for several years. This happened nearly every single time. Whether I thought the opposite or not! You got to keep moving constantly. I was trying to move anyway. Perhaps if I stayed in Tustin a week longer I could move my arm and hand better today. I'm still improving 9 years later. I 'm always deciding how much you can work out without can do without doing too much. What is too much and make myself pop again. I had no advice on this especially at the beginning. Oops, I'm skipping around again! Grown man coming through!

Every day I was still so nervous and hated sudden sounds. My heart was beating out of my chest. My breastbone and ribs hurt. Was it my heart or what Day after day anxiety building not knowing if I was going to live or die? This was really scary stuff.

Another dreary stay was in order. Sure go on in to emergency and get the automatic invite for another hospital admission. Rat barf! I was nervous even though it was my primary hospital where I spent the first three days in the Intensive care after the stroke. Crapola, I hate this being 46 and wondering what is wrong with my heart!!!! What haven't they told me? This was only a few weeks after my 22 day hospy trek. You got to love it! Test that I don't remember to well but they happened and days of waiting! Why? No information from folks. The nurse from my intensive visit 5 weeks before (right after the stroke) stopped by and was amazed at how well I was doing and how much weight I had lost.

THAT DARN 1,200 CALORIES A DAY DIET was spawning to the 1,800 calories a day diet sure continued my weakness beyond belief. Of course the stroke was the real reason why! Finally, after worry, stress and in need of "calm me down" medication I was relieved not by medication but the OK to go home. Of course the doctors argued and were in disagreement as usual. This would keep me nervous for years and in anticipation of some pending down like a huge asteroid hitting the earth. I have needed for 25 days to calm down.

Somehow, I was still on overdrive!!! I was normal but still with so much wrong with me including frayed nerves. Did I ever get something too calm me down? No, No, No!!!!! Never would. This is really why and what I needed going to emergency in the first place. I could continue to walk with the cane stuck in that peanut butter carpet in my Mother's apartment, one step at a time.

Home on the Range

It was now time for about six weeks of a few times a week home physical therapy and Jerry was his name-o. This was covered from my insurance. He was great and shot me in the right direction of exercises to continue strength, endurance and movement back. I slowly got more energy and endured the frustrations of all parties concerned.

I was Walking with the four pronged cane with less difficulty. I did not need the wheelchair in the house or for short walks. That wheelchair stayed folded up in the corner near the TV. It was a rental and began driving me more bonkers and more frustrated the better I got. I didn't need it anymore. It sat there by the TV that I watched most the day annoying me. Somehow I thought Mom was still thinking I would be in the wheelchair forever. I would be forever a nuisance to her. I didn't think she noticed I didn't use it anymore for weeks. She continued to talk like I would be wheeled around to ballgames and whatever. Her comments were all taken the wrong way by me. You know the unperceptive negative way. This was the most popular way that I usually thought.

The last visit by a physical therapist at home was by another dude. The switch may have been for certain "news". I was weak but a bit stronger per week. My balance was pathetic but slightly better all the time. It was time for physical therapy in Fountain Valley. I had about 12 sessions covered on my insurance. They had weights and all kind of stuff. Eventually that let me climb a small grassy knoll outside. It keeps popping up. I made it up and done on my own with the cane. But still.....as Kirk would say I didn't feel really human.

After months of begging my computer expert brother to simply set up my unassembled computer for me, I mustered up the strength and pain bending down to set it up me. I could check my email and research my stroke. I finally reread the one form I got from the Doctor for the therapist. I thought it said "routine CVA" It said "Pontine CVA"!!! This is the first time, 3 months after the stroke that I knew the bleed/stroke was in the pons. I researched many sites online about Pontine infract strokes and found that I was fortunate to be alive. "One of the most devastating strokes known to mankind" was a common medical website description. "Invariably fatal" was another. I printed up perhaps a 100 pages of data including all my reality of symptoms post stroke. I still have them today. This wasn't a nice feeling to my soul. But still I could say to death ears "SEE"!!!!

I was still so nervous, high strung, revved up with no place to go!!!! This is 3 months after the stroke. Sleeping poorly at night was my specialty in life. Slowly I became better. OMG, I was reliving my childhood, only worse, way worse, way, way worse!!!!I was an adult and not retarded, brain dead or stupid as I was always perceived by me to be. I still seemed more functional than my brother and mother. I had to get better enough to get away from them. Such close quarters were agonizing torture for me. The loudness of everything was destroying my head. My mom was so deaf. The loudness of fan noises was like being drilled at the dentist with no nova cane. No nova cane what I did one time as a kid to save my parents money. The mental struggle of having what was perceived by me as the exact opposite of "care takers" compassionate people. I did not want to be there in the worst way. I had month after month of tedious ridiculous existence. This sucked to me as bad as with my life in peril in the hospital.

How could I survive this and have a somewhat semi-normal life? After all, I didn't feel human yet after 3 or 4 months from the stroke. I bumbled and stumbled with whipped down dignity and sense of self. I couldn't be a "self" or have rights, feelings or anything against the overlords. I think you get it. How sweet it wasn't to live like this. No wonder

I had a feeling of doom and gloom even today. This creeps in or oozes from my soul even today 10 years later, I want to be left alone with no interruptions or rules by others. Get out the violins. I have turned into that pussy that my fencing teammate in College Joe expounded about. I was a pussy in my mind. Not a champion or a survivor or little feeling of accomplishment during these months and months after the stroke.

The Bally gym was within staggering distance just over a half mile away from apartment. Actually I drove. I started driving after 5 months from the stroke. I only drove to the store and gym. No more than about a mile at a time. This was way ahead of the loose time lime of improvement. Sure it was like I was off in the head, but I was extra careful and only managed to tear up my passenger side mirror on the narrowest enclosed parking space that you can dream of. Hello Gaff tape!

Bally Gym yeah!!!!!!!!!!!!!!I started going there to improve more and more. Wow certain social contact. I was seeing actual people. I went very often and was so weak especially on the right side. Wow! There are actual pretty women that move around. This was a 1,000 times even if that is enough a billion times better world than my everyday living! My endurance was terrible after all I didn't feel quit human yet.

We were still in that one bedroom apartment. That is my Mother's apartment, her inflexible rules and ways of doing things. There we were, my brother Paul, Mother and me all there 7 months after the stroke. We than moved in the same complex to a 2 bedroom apartment. Several of my friends graciously helped me move. Chris, Rad, Steve and Rene I think. Somehow Steve's six pack of beer was seen evil by my Mom, and not how grateful she should have been for the help moving all her things. My God a 6 pack for 4 guys isn't a lot of swilling! The conditions were somewhat improved with space but this time was all blurred with many arguments with little of them by me. Misery and being miserable were expected by all. Suffering more than I had to be all part of the process for someday leaving Tara! I just wanted peace and peace of mind and finally felt human after 7 months from the stroke. I knew I was good for nothing and that nobody could live with me and I was destined for nothing! My pleading and begging for less noise which was so hard on my head and my still fragile half shattered nerves would never happen living with my Mom. You know I was considered the evil child by mom (so opposite in reality) and I was always blamed for 95% of things that prodigal son Paul did. He set me up on purpose. He got off on watching me blamed and suffering.

It would be 7 more months of 2 bedrooms, 3 people living together that shouldn't be. We all saw the world and neutral space differently. This will be 14 months since the stroke living crowded and miserable.

Sweet Home Anaheim

Sweet home Anaheim! I was moving by myself! I was so beaten down mentally. I felt I could do it and spend the $800 month rent to get away from all the crap. Sure it was a half mile away from that two bedroom prison, but I had some quiet and the ability to try and improve mentally. Yes, I had made great gains in the brain cognitive, but that feeling of freedom was no in the air. The air would be breathed and shared by thousands of cock-roaches, but that's months from now. I was still shaking and moving but now I would be a few hundred yards from the gym. I could get my right arm over my head maybe 6 inches from a full overhead stretch equally my left arm. I was after all, on my way baby. I was pissing it all away and treading deeper and deeper in debt. I still believed that I could pay it all back.

Wishing I could pay it all back anyway. Frugal living besides $800 rent for my older but huge one bedroom apartment. Financial ruin, hope for a cool job and some hot woman loving me was beyond the stars to me.

I stumbled and bumbled. I put my shirt on backwards nearly every time. Frustrated daily I had to switch the shirt to the front. This was eating at my self-esteem. I dropped my medication with my good side nearly every day. I spilled coffee on the rug, slipped on wet floors and slipped on dry floors. Still I pushed ahead. I had some quiet time with my soon to be cockroach infested apartment. It did free but heavily impaired but improving all the time. I was very lonely but what else was new? I lived there 9 months building strength and coordination to move to Reno Nevada and cheaper rent. Still going deeper in debt daily and hearing the wrong things from Mother and Brother always fighting.

Reno Baby

It was time to get out of Dodge and leave the greater Orange County/Los Angeles area and get away from all my troubles in L.A. It was August 2004 and nearly 2 years after the stroke. I was still weak and uncoordinated on the "so called" left side of my body. Weak and pretty impaired in the hand and foot on the right side. My brain stills a mess but less so every month. My friend Big Bob and Son Trevor were waiting for me to move into their apartment complex. What an ordeal physical to ready for the move as I had to throw out things that should have been gone through and thrown out for the last 15 years.

I continued to work the parts a lot, but needed to sign up for gym support too. 24 hour fitness came to the rescue. Everything kept slowly improving over the next few years. I wanted to start fencing again even though I was overweight and impaired on the right side. So I would fencelike an old man! I fenced as much as money would allow starting in 2006. I was OK considering my vision/reaction time/balance/overall weakness hampered me. I was left handed and I just had to do it.

I loved fencing so. I improved every year since. I had the habit of my right side seizing up after a while when I fenced and many fences like a brick days over the years. I called my seizing up imploding or "Chernobyl" but it are the muscles messing up called spasticity. Of course this tired me out instantly. My whole body would wear out. I get fencing some every year since as money would allow. My confidence nearly shattered even though my body would be much improved. I quit dropping my medication with the good hand!

I was on Social Security with my retirement pot at zero so this was my Social Security. I was on several types of benefits like Medicare and finally in 2010 a HUD apartment with cheap rent. I could of tried to get in 2005 but I was to stupid and insecure or reluctant to find out how. This cost me many thousands of dollars in extra rent. I am less reluctant all the time but still blow chunks on some things because I'm dense and reluctant. Fear or some facsimile thereof has cost me a ton of money and happiness in my life. Reluctant to change and get out of a rut it almost cost me my life from the stroke in 2002.

Still, I worked to improve my vision, alertness, focus, strength, mobility...... You get it everything. Frustrated and down and happy sometimes I have had a boring life so far in Reno from 2004to 2012. I have come so far!

You have structure and commitment to forge back to keep improving! I went to the gym 250 times a year for a few years and downsized with longer better workouts to 200 a year. Fencing mixed in too! I was frustrated beyond belief with the hurdles, pain in joints, the stumbling and stumbling. I was frustrated how sensitive I was to things and unaware of things. Somehow I couldn't think things through enough. I didn't ask enough questions a draw back from my childhood and whole life. I didn't trust the right things. The light bulbs in my head came on and sometimes out again only to fire back up. Physically I said "wow so this is what it feels like to be a man". I revise that wow all the time every year!!! I figured out eventually how to make my social security money last longer. If I would have had help I would have had less frustration, more clarity, and saved

time and tons of money. Yet despite all this I kept going.
Reno Baby!!!

HITLER HAD A FAT ASS

The dreaded self-body image and others image of you
may be very different. Most of us feel pressured by
society, TV and so on to look good. Really for me being
reasonably lean is healthier with so many things being
easier to do. A nice cardiovascular base is part of this.
Just how do others see us? Let's take a look at Hitler. His
"body" was overlooked by the German's of his day. You
will notice all his propaganda film only shows him from
his best angles where he is more "dominate". However,
this was true of just about all leaders including Churchill
and Roosevelt. Is it there henchmen that make sure of

this or do? Did they have a clue about their weaknesses? Did Hitler know he had a fat ass? Did people notice this when they saw him in person? If they did, it didn't matter. I didn't realize that Hitler had a fat ass until a few years ago.

I saw a documentary on the history channel examining Hitler's illnesses disguised by his "home type movies. Footage shot by his doctor and other home movie film shows Hitler's trembling hand in his later years and his fat ass! We finally got to see him from the back without camouflage. His hand trembling was probably from early Parkinson's and/or late stage syphilis. However, I noticed then that he had a fat ass compared to "his physic". Of course, perhaps I am the one who is crazy. Perhaps just a few of this think this. But the odds are that you haven't seen the "revealing" film footage. Yes, one the most evil men in history had a fat ass besides the so called partial Jewish lineage. No one seems to care now that he had a fat ass. Did they care then? Was everybody rightfully tunneled on the evil of this man or following him blindly? Yes Virginia, fat is blind!

Some of my points are Hitler rose above his fat ass and became a Fuhrer and executed millions. Was his fat ass a catalyst or didn't he know? Anyway, you get the idea. Self-image, what others think of us is likely to be different. Everybody has an Opinion. What do the majority think? If millions polled think you are very thin than your own self-image that you are "fat" perhaps maybe skewed. Let's take a look at my personal numbers leading into my stroke:

Key: Good HDL cholesterol over 34 and Bad LDL under 130 Want total under 200

You want triglycerides under 200 and 150 even better.

Triglycerides = Tri on chart.

Jan 2001 My 197 total cholesterol, Good HDL 47/ bad LDL 98. Tri 258

255 Aug 2002

250 Sept 2002 198 total cholesterol, about 250 Triglycerides

? Nov 2002 134 total Cholesterol HDL 29 and LDL 58, Tri 237.

218 Dec 2002

219 Feb 2003 125 total cholesterol HDL 30 and LDL 58. Tri 187

224 April 2004

233 March 2005

227.5 May 2005 150 total cholesterol HDL 38 and LDL BAD 58 Tri 294 way up!

235 Nov 2005

239.5 Jan 3, 2005

234 Jan 2006

217 Mar 2006

190 Sept 2006

188 Sept 2006

189 Oct 2006

191 Nov 2006 86 Total Cholesterol with Good HDL too low at about 28

189.5 Dec 2006

189 Jan 2007

199 June 2007. 119 total cholesterol good HDL 36 and bad LDL 62. Tri 104

206.5 Sept 2008

188 April 2009

194.5 Aug 2009 143 total Cholesterol

192 Jan 2009

193.5 Nov 2009

194.5 Mar 2010 145 total cholesterol. Good HDL 33 and bad LDL 69. Tri 213

208.5 Aug 2010

What a mess. Let's decipher this stuff. Overall, notice the big difference in numbers affected by my diet. This means you can change these too. I should point out that I gained muscle over the years and peaks in 2008 and 2010 were about the same belly button waist line. The ensuing low in 2009 from 2006 had a smaller waist. Now it is time for my actual diet. Trumpets please! It takes discipline but you are not staving yourself. It is a slower to lose weight diet. Since I was exercising I ate a decent amount of protein. I was usually around 250 to 600 calories of protein a day. 1 gram of protein is 4 calories. It was low in fat in general being 150 to 700 calories of fat. 1 gram of fat is 9 calories. My total calories averaged, averaged mine you, about 2,200 to 2,300 a day. I lost 51 pounds in 38 weeks. I lost way more a month at first since I weighed more. This is about 11 pounds a month down to about 2 ½ pounds a month. The calories per day could vary a lot. 1,200 to 3,200 let's say. Remember I averaged about 2,300 calories eaten a day over the 51 weeks.

I had no conventional fast food except pizza every week or two. I ate basically no sweets. I did have a lot of buttered popcorn at the movies every other week. I was in control of it all. I charted all calories every day. I pretty much still do it 5 years later 90% of the time. I charted daily protein, fat. Total calories eat, exercise burn (estimate), and differential gain or loss every single day. I recommend a gram scale in determining weight of portions that you need to determine. In the food where the content is shown on container you can figure % of each. Otherwise I use the Internet to determine calorie values of fat/protein/overall. It should be noted that even with a gram scale and prudent work every day you may still be inaccurate. You might under estimate butter products/sugar and so on. I read how many calories were in a microwavable popcorn bag for example. The box is confusing and unclear in some items.

If you have poor control of calorie counting because you are on the road or eating in restaurants you should eat in restaurants that show total calories and at least fat. Fat reduction is critical. I eat two to three times less fat in my diet when dieting. This lowers Triglycerides and helps cholesterol somewhat. I got my cholesterol from about 198 at the time of the stroke down, way down to 86 after losing 51 pounds. This was the lowest or close overall reading that the doctor has ever seen. That's right 86.The good cholesterol was low. The protective cholesterol is the good cholesterol. I should add that I was 12 pounds lighter when I started this diet than I was before the stroke. I fluctuated weighing for three years between 220 to 240 pounds after the stroke. I started the diet at 238 1/2 and ended at 187.5. I am 5 foot 11 inches. I was 250 pounds at the time of the stroke.

Try not to weigh yourself very often while dieting. When you do weigh yourself do it in the morning first thing before you eat and drink. Relieve yourself first and note if it is before bowel movement. Your weight will be more accurate this way. This can cut down on "that mid-day weight fluctuations". You will get "happier more accurate" readings. Remember if you ate a lot the day before with a lot of salt this will add more weight for the next day reading. This food is mostly still in your system. By not weighing yourself often you don't get hung up and daily odd fluctuations and get discouraged. Each day leads to the big picture and the goal. I am very good at estimating my weight even if I do not weigh myself for weeks and weeks.

How to figure the calories you burn to your weight? Like I said keep it simple. If you weigh 200 pounds you burn around 2,000 to 2,400 calories a day. This is doing nothing, no ugly exercise. It depends what you read and what your own personal metabolism is. I probably over estimated for years what my base calorie burn rate for my weight was. It was probably really 2,200 or 2,300 not 2,400 for 200 pounds like I thought. This can add up to an error of 3/4 to 1 1/2 pounds a month. Is this a coincidence? That I gain about a pound a month on average when I'm not dieting? Therefore, each day you figure your exercise burn and mount of calories and add to your weight base rate calories. For example, 200 pounds is 2,300 (active good metabolism). Plus 300 exercise calories equals 2,500. So 2,500 would be that day's burn. Hopefully, you ate less than 2,500 calories that day. A pound of weight is about 4,000 calories.

So if you want to lose an average of one pound a week you need to lose about 571 calories a day. Round it off if you want to but this is my basic simple premise. Therefore, to keep on track for the day of 2,500 total burn calories you should eat say "1,930 calories". Remember your daily burn will fluctuate with your exercise. You may burn 800 calories one day exercising and 200 another. You really need to make a good attempt at your calorie burn from exercising. Use a lot of gym machines that tell you calorie burn or estimate from charts you can track from the Internet.

One of my strengths is estimating calorie exercise burn. I've confused myself by now! As your weight drops adjust your weight calorie burn. You burn about 12 calories with every pound you lose. If you weigh ten less pounds than your daily calorie burn is about 120 calories less a day. In a 30 day month is 3,600 calories or 9/10Th's of a pound. You will less weight as you lose if you don't decrease your daily calories or exercise more. So keep track of these daily numbers to see how accurate you are and to make adjustments for weight loss.

Anyway, it has 100% worked for me. It takes a little effort and commitment. Make a real commitment to lose weight and be healthier! I know you're asking me not to bore you. Yeah, yeah, yeah. She loves you. Make short term, medium term and long term weight lose goals. The short term goals can be adjusted if need be every few weeks or so. Short term goals should be weight loss in is for a week or two. You can make adjustments to these short term goals in order to make your medium term goal. Remember it is easy to overestimate the amount of calories you are burning from exercise added to your metabolism/current weight amount of burned calories.

I try and simply this some. Sure the reality maybe a little different for you but you can get pretty close keeping it somewhat simple. A good medium term goal is your amount of weight loss for a month or two. Write down your goal weight for that date in the future. You now need to figure how many calories a day below what you are burning to achieve this. By all means do what works for you.

The long term goal is the weight you want to achieve in X amount of the time. Say 51 pounds like my first big goal oriented weight loss.

Sample daily calorie chart:

Date/ Total eaten/ Protein/ fat/ exercise burn/ Basal burn/ total burn/ difference

1/2,030/ 428 /362/ 300 /2,300 /2,600/ (570) A loss of 570 calories.

Your actual calories ate for me in a day bounces around and calories burned per day bounces around and yes I even have some slight weight gain days, that pizza or buttered popcorn but the vast majority are weight lose days during a diet. I'm not really suffering or starving myself or trying to lose too much weight too fast. I eat a few "bad things" for me, but not a lot. Keep on track and enjoy the discipline! The main thing for me was to really reduce fat intake by two to three fold. Cut down on fat. Eat low fat or nonfat substitutes. No fat frozen yogurt is great. I eat no fat hot dogs. I like them. If you can't make it make your hot dogs and no fat hot dogs and cut them in half and eat a half and half. Eat lower fat margarines so on! Just do it.

You want to lose weight don't you? I drink very little regular soft drinks. I drink by accident a real soft drink with those 150 calories of sugar every once in a while. I don't drink. If you are a boozer cut back. You get it. If you're in these categories or perceived by most in these categories change a bit. "Boozers, losers, snoozers and schmoozers".

A small bit at first if you have to. Make it happen. A schmuck like I did. My second diet I lost 19 pounds that I had gained 19 pounds over a few years. I lost an average of a pound a week again. So try to be healthier and reach goals and don't worry about every ounce or whether you think you might have a fat ass. Do something about it. Remember Hitler had a Fat ass

Déjà Vu

Déjà Vu! It's seems to be happening to me a lot the last six months. Is it that my life repeating stuff? I figure out many similar things from the past, but a few lately! OMG, these are from dreams I had. They were vivid moments of the reoccurring dreams. In fact, I knew lately as it was happening, those short clips as you will that they were from the dream. Bizarre! Here are the two most vivid examples!

My Uncle Bob passed away in March 2012. I drove down from Reno to Orange County California for the Memorial Service. My cousin Jan flew down from Canada for the service. She treated me to Disneyland with her the day after the service. I swear I recognized segments of the day from a dream I had several times a few years before. I couldn't figure out in the dream why I was at Disneyland with just Jan. Did I do a similar thing 10 to 20 years ago?

A few things seemed exact to the segments in my dream. Two Asian fellows ahead of us in a "Small, Small World" line took our photo. He was the Asian on the right who did the same things. The way the photo was framed with Jan and I tiny in the bottom of picture was exactly the same as the dream.

When we were leaving and the tram was taking us back to the parking lot the folks behind us had the exact talk, a guy they know hooking up with about 6 or 7 coworkers as I expected to happen. They were placed in the near empty Tram exactly where they were in the dream. Jan was on my right as was the dream. The wording from the guy was precisely like the dream. I briefly looked back and really only saw the gal who spoke maybe 3% of the time during several minutes. Like the dream. Jan and I didn't speak during these few minutes.

Am I loony? Tunes? The "hooking up" phrase he kept saying was so right on? Jan's clothes seemed right to me too. Did a similar thing happen to me many years before? Strange! Bizarre! Did I live long enough and repeat certain things?

I figure so many things out, like meeting a person a year before within a few days? Is my head clogged from remembering similar things? I must tell you those segments from the dream were spot on to reality!!!! I have few vivid dreams that I remember and reflect over several times over the years. Perhaps that hole in my head is taking over!

I'm jumping ahead to a little over 3 weeks later. It was time for me to fly to Los Angeles and fence at the Memorial in Pasadena. OMG. There was so many Déjà Vu moments and right out of a vivid dream I had a few times. The Travelodge in Pasadena was the exact room and floor. The old man that I could view in the Jacuzzi 30 yards away for a few seconds. Exactly the same I felt. The noisy air conditioner in my room was the same. The couple having sex in the next room which was amplified by the double door leading to my room was the same. How weird? I remember the market nearby. I remember the exact parking garage at Pasadena City College, the exact trimmed football field and fences by the gym were we fenced.

I was praying somebody was there to let me in the back door isolated from the main door. Thank god she opened the door saving me another half mile walk trekking my gear. The place I sat in the gym was the same. The placement of the armorer location was the same. One Man's room closed seemed the same. Feeling tired and out of shape the same. The talk to Chuck was the same. Somehow, I must have fenced or directed there 20 or 30 years ago. I can't remember doing it. Did I? It could not be since the stroke in 2002.

How could this be so much the same? This was only 30 hours into trip. The rent car and Travelodge by Lax for the second night of my trip the same. It was the same room. Not being able to find it for 10 minutes. While checking in, the same guy on the phone with a clueless guy trying to find shuttle at LAX. Playing to me like a repeat movie. My god the walk to store was the same

How could I stay there before? I have been in Reno eight years. No way had I stayed there when my brother/mom still lived in Los Angeles. I stayed at Randi's after. Was there a short trip that I stayed there? When I flew back a few times I did not need a motel. I don't remember staying in a Travelodge let alone 2 Travelodge's before. You get the idea.

Oh yeah guests at lodge were checking me out like I were a celebrity at breakfast the day I left at the Travelodge. Perhaps they thought I was Jack Black. This 10 second sequence in my dream seemed exact. 5, 10 or 20 seconds of the dream splattered with reality.

It was all bizarre to me. Anyway, I thought I'd tell you. So we have established that I must be getting old. Are events that similar happening in my past?

In The Beginning

Well, we won't start there but I was often picked last in gym class a lot before I could prove myself as worthy! I was blamed for thousands of things I didn't do and yes you can play those violins again!

Let's skip ahead to when I started fencing. I was 19 and a sophomore in College. Hey, I saw it the before in the sport's section of the student paper of CSULB (Long Beach State). I liked the small section of the World Book encyclopedia as a kid. They had hard cover encyclopedias then. So I got the balls and walked in to try out the fencing team. Coach Jo Redmon was at the helm. I would be put into Epee which seemed to suit my palate anyway. I was also taking the beginning foil class concurrently.

I had many wonderful times with teammates and fencing my three years left at Long Beach State. It was a fantastic growing experience and was definitely what I needed!!!!!!!! I was super-fast and athletic and offensive minded. A lot of trial by error for many years along with some coaching by Redmon and teammates and I was really good! I got better in thinking and better at my skills and was excellent by time I graduated in 1978.

I beat my first Olympian in an AFLA (now USFA) tournament. He was USA 1976 Olympian Wayne Johnson. This was in 1978. I super jacked up and coming up with multi action attacks pushed to a 4 to 0 lead. First to score one to 5 wins. He in frustration finally attacked hard and powerful put I was able to pull out a double touch. This means we were both scored on within 1/25 of a second. With a double touch it made the score 5 to 1 from 4 to 0. Yes!!!!!!!!!!!!!!!!!!!!!!!! I won 5 to 1 against a current world class Epeeist!!!!!!!!!!!!! One thing for sure I had an extremely fast attack system and was very hard to stop when things were going right.

I was second place in over 20 fencers a year half into fencing. I beat some of the really great ones. This was the Orange Coast Divisional Championships. This covered Long Beach CA, Orange County and some of San Diego. It included San Diego in some of the years.

I loved this annual qualifier for Nationals as I won it the next three years losing just one or two Bouts against about 40 bouts. There were always about 20 competing. I beat Junior Olympians and some of the best in USA every year. Somehow I always had focused on this tourney and was confident for it.

I was sick the next year and ended up 4Th as I was slowing down on the amount of fencing I did. I won again the next year after taking the next 11 months off. I started fencing again one month before the event. For 4 titles in 5 years! Not bad for a tweaked mind.

I had perceived apathy from friends and family. I went many years with no one seeing me fence. This apathy to me leads to depression and giving up the sport. A handful of people saw me compete in my college years but the next 9 years nobody saw me fence. Perhaps I was right. However, I was much more humble and shy then and didn't say how much I was suffering. The way I was and still am is very seldom ask for help, ask for clarification. Never did I raise my hand in school to ask a question. I was afraid to not know something and felt unworthy even more if I showed weakness. I needed to be right to be worthy and as good as others.

I was and still socially retarded in thinking I'm not desirable and could very seldom ask a girl out or "god forbid" ask her phone number. The stroke and its problems and the "gift that keeps on giving" pushed up these barriers again. I'm so nice that I can't see anyone giving there number for business either. I have wasted so much time and effort until the light bulbs go on and melt away these barriers. In fact, the prettier the girl the more I think she can't like me. Gosh, I have lived a much less rich life due to these handicaps in my mind. I can have the confidence to beat Olympians but I can't ask for a number even for business. What a pussy I am!!!!!!!!!!!!!!!!!!!!!!I still blow chunks and shake my head on the table today. I am so shy in this regard. No wonder I'm not married or have a girlfriend. My fragile head!!!!!!!!!!!!!!!

There was an old TV commercial from the early 70's I think that showed a wimp who wanted Pennzoil from the Gas guy, but he was too afraid to ask. Finally he yelled out "I want Pennzoil!" I was still afraid of the world all my life through my twenties. I fenced less and less every year in my later twenties. I competed in nothing but a few North American Cups and no other tourneys. I still did well but not great as before in one and after three or four more years of no competitions I did another Cup. Nobody around me noticed or asked how come you're not fencing? I was burned out on no one caring or seeing fence. It was way too painful. I slowly over years gained weight, worked too much at low pay and had poor self-esteem as always. I no longer was lean and fenced and was great at it. I had poor self-esteem then too!

I did not fence at all from 1992 to the time of the stroke in 2002. A nice guy with low self-esteem like I was easy prey to take advantage of!!! I have learned to stand up for myself more but still I have some mind freezes for years and I cost myself more happiness, money and peace of mind.

I'm Back

I forget sometimes how much more aware and confident I am in so many ways more than I was even the year before. Tragic happenings like my Mom passing in October 2011 and my uncle in March 2012 kept me down for months. This of course led to more judgment errors. Hind sight tells you should have done things different to help your personal happiness and to be less lonely. The reality of the moment and road blocks in a few key areas of my mind stopped me from a better life. I'm talking psychological scars and road blocks and the fear or reluctant to "make it happen "have impaired me so just like the physical impairments.

I am still improving my hand slowly and am stronger, better balance, less impaired person all the time. I am still improving my mental well-being also. Every so often I have Epiphanies that clear up issues in my road block filled head. I may need to anguish heavy for a week running many better things that could have happened to me and angry at my stupidity. But my head is so much clearer on everything. I have had too much free time to day dream and ponder whether it is nice or negative. My negative self-talk is so much less now it in itself is mind boggling. I can't day dream my life away. Not now! My health is excellent right now, knock on wood.

Have more fun, focus on what you want, don't ponder, be reluctant on short changing yourself on a more fulfilling life. I can't just save for a rainy day because I can die before that. I can't spend like an idiot either. Balance it all juggle it all. Things are not like my spinning poor balance used to be!!!Life is not bad right now. A few more tweaks and OMG!!!!

Ring the bells even if no one hears and if few care I blessed with life and some loved ones and some friends. Sure it can be better, but most of say that. So keep moving and trying to improve and if you slip to a rut find out how to get out. Do the things you like and make it happen. I like some discipline and structure in my life. I am happier like this and it is a great foundation for everyday living for me.

I don't have that beautiful wife or girlfriend but I don't have the problems that can arise from that. I am a nice guy with incredible character and loyalty! All those grand adjectives are over looked by many. Be undaunted! I plod forward ever hoping for a better life. I am better armed now physically and mentally to make that happen!!!! The road blocks are coming down!!!!

Remember how I told you I beat fencing Olympians when I was young? Well it happened again. Twice in my age group at 2012 Men's Epee fencing age 50-59. This time there former Olympians but still near the top in the USA in my age group. I fenced two former Olympians and two wins for me. I had not beaten a top rated fencer since my stroke. I beat two super duper top ranked fencers. Jim Carpenter was a former Epee fencing Olympian and was 4Th ranked the in USA at the time of Nationals in 50 to 59. Rankings are determined by points in your best two results in three tournaments. They are Two North American Cups and the USA National Championships. I beat Carpenter in direct elimination 10 to 9 in the first round. This dropped from 4Th and a trip to Austria on the world team to 8Th which is the 4Th alternate? By golly I did it. I fenced like I did 30 years ago!

I placed 32 of 69 fencers but I finally did very well in competition against the best fencers in my age group and some of the best in my age group in the world. I was so excited from this and only had a short rest and couldn't get my pulse down from a hummingbird rate in time for my next bout against another outstanding fencer. It was an amazing fast paced final 20 seconds with a lot of action as I was trying to tie the score. I rushed at him with nearly no time and barely missed his arm and then he hit me with perhaps two tenths of a second left if that. I almost tied it for overtime!

Backing up to the earlier seeding round robin pool of seven, I beat three times Olympian and Team Gold medalist from the Modern Pentathlon which includes Epee fencing MacieJ Czyzowicz 5 to 3. By golly I did it!

My friends were amazed how awesome I was and of course had seen me when I was pathetic too good. They never saw me have awesome bouts before! Their mouths were open in amazement!

I see a much less of a struggle to fence in the future as my fencing future looks bright again. It is beyond normal comprehension to come back from nearly nothing. I have impairments in my right hand and fingers still and my right arm is weak. Kinks in the armor in spots but I can say the brain is improving all the time and the body is improving all the time. I have scrambled brains and poor grammar. I'm Back.

Let me tell you about two times when I prayed really hard and emotional. It was a self-pity type of prayer. Now I'm not religious but I felt compelled to pray on these two occasions. I took care of my friend's dog for a while in January 1998. I prayed to have a pet that I could love. Of course this is easily fixed by just making the effort to get a pet. The next evening a parrot walked in my balcony door in Huntington Beach where I was living. I searched for the owner with no avail so I kept him. This is Virgil. I still have him 15 years later!

The next time I prayed really hard was nearly 5 years later. I prayed to quit drinking, lose weight, change careers and get my whole life together. The next night I had the stroke. I got what I asked for. I wasn't specific enough! I am probably better off today now than I would have been without the stroke. It has been so hard to get here. I'm still improving.

I am way more emotional and improved in so many ways. You know you got to keep moving and try! You know I'm still making the delusion true!

Made in the USA
Middletown, DE
08 April 2022

63871378R00070